LIFE CYCLE OF A...

Dog

Revised and Updated

Angela Royston

Heinemann Library
Chicago, Illinois

©2001, 2009 Heinemann Library
an imprint of Capstone Global Library, LLC
Chicago, Illinois

Edited by Adrian Vigliano, Diyan Leake, and Harriet Milles
Designed by Kimberly R. Miracle and Tony Miracle
Original illustrations © Capstone Global Library Limited 2001, 2009
Illustrated by Alan Fraser
Picture research by Tracy Cummins and Heather Mauldin
Originated by Chroma Graphics (Overseas) Pte. Ltd.
Printed in China by South China Printing Company Ltd.

13 12 11 10 09
10 9 8 7 6 5 4 3 2 1

New edition ISBNs: 978 1 4329 2525 3 (hardcover)
                    978 1 4329 2542 0 (paperback)

The Library of Congress has cataloged the first edition as follows:
Royston, Angela.
  Life cycle of a dog / by Angela Royston.
    p. cm.
  Includes bibliographical references (p.) and index.
      Summary: Introduces the life cycle of a dog, using a golden retriever as an example and describing various stages of her life, from newborn puppy to adult dog having puppies of her own.
        ISBN 1-57572-209-7 (lib. Bdg.)
  1. Dogs—Life cycles—Juvenile literature. [1. Dogs.]
  I. Title.
  SF426.5.R69 2000
  636.752'7—dc21
              99-046854

Acknowledgments
The author and publishers are grateful to the following for permission to reproduce copyright material: Age Fotostock p. 18 (© SuperStock); Ardea pp. 6 (© John Daniels), 7 (© John Daniels), 9 (© John Daniels), 10 (© John Daniels), 11 (© John Daniels), 15 (© Jean Michel Labat), 19 (© Jean Michel Labat), 28 top left (© John Daniels), 28 top right (© John Daniels); Corbis p. 4 (© Tim Davis); Getty pp12 (© G.K. Hart/Vikki Hart), 24 (© Chase Jarvis); istockphoto p. 27 (© Monique Rodriguez); Minden Pictures p. 23 (© Mitsuaki Iwago); National Geographic Stock pp. 26 (© Jason Edwards), 29 bottom (© Jason Edwards); PhotoEdit pp. 17 (© Mark Richards), 21 (© Nancy Sheehan), 22 (© Nancy Sheehan); Photolibrary pp. 14 (© Frank Siteman), 16 (© John Giustina), 28 top right (© Oxford Scientific); Shutterstock pp. 5 (© Micimakin), 8 (© Paul Clarke), 13 (© Martin Valigursky), 20 (© Aleksey Ignatenko), 25 (© Tonis Valing), 28 bottom (© Martin Valigursky), 29 top left (© Micimakin).

Cover photograph of a golden retriever reproduced with permission of Getty Images (© Photographer's Choice/G.K. Hart/Vikki Hart).

We would like to thank Michael Bright for his invaluable help in the preparation of this book.

Every effort has been made to contact copyright holders of any material reproduced in this book. Any omissions will be rectified in subsequent printings if notice is given to the publisher.

Contents

Some words are shown in bold, **like this**. You can find out what they mean by looking in the glossary.

Meet the Dogs

This photo shows a basset hound, a golden retriever, and a chihuahua.

There are hundreds of different kinds of dogs. They come in different colors and sizes.

Newborn

6 weeks

2 months

Golden retrievers are very good as pet dogs.

This book tells you about the life of a **female** golden retriever. She has floppy ears and a long tail. She began life as a tiny puppy.

1 year

3 years

8 years

Newborn

The mother dog licks her puppies as they are born.

The mother dog has given birth to a **litter**. The little **female** puppy is the last to be born. She has lots of brothers and sisters.

Newborn

6 weeks

2 months

Now the newborn puppy is clean and dry. She cannot see or hear, but she can feel and smell. She smells her mother and the other puppies in the litter.

A puppy's paws look very big compared to its body size!

1 Week

The puppy's pink nose has now turned black.

The puppy feeds on her mother's milk. She has to push her way through her brothers and sisters to find a **teat** to suckle from.

Newborn

6 weeks

2 months

The smallest puppy in a **litter** is called the runt.

The puppies feed and grow bigger. They still cannot stand, but they snuggle up together and sleep.

1 year   3 years   8 years

6 Weeks

A puppy's eyes open when it is about 10 days old.

The puppy's eyes have opened, and she can see and hear. Her legs are strong now, and she plays and explores.

Newborn

6 weeks

2 months

Puppies play-fight and then cuddle up together for a nap.

She plays with her brothers and sisters. Sometimes she pretends to fight with one of them. In this way the puppies learn who is stronger.

1 year   3 years   8 years

2 Months

Puppies should have their shots before they go outside.

A **veterinarian** checks the puppy all over and gives her a special **shot**. The shot will protect her from getting diseases.

Newborn

6 weeks

2 months

Dogs can smell better than they can see.

The puppy can now go outside for the first time. Everything is strange. The puppy has a good sense of smell and uses it to explore.

1 year

3 years

8 years

3 Months

The dog leaves her mother and goes to a new owner. She begins to eat solid food now instead of milk. The food contains meat and grain.

A new puppy needs a lot of looking after.

Newborn

6 weeks

2 months

It's good for a dog to feel happy around other dogs.

Food gives the dog **energy** and keeps her healthy. Exercise makes her muscles stronger. She plays with other dogs she meets outside.

1 year

3 years

8 years

1 Year

Large, active dogs need lots of exercise.

The dog is now fully grown. She has lots of **energy**. When her owner throws a stick, she runs and brings it back.

Newborn

6 weeks

2 months

Retrievers can be **trained** to do tasks and help people. Some are specially trained to be guide dogs. They help people with sight problems find their way around.

This guide dog makes sure it is safe for its owner to cross the street.

1 year

3 years

8 years

3 Months Later

This vet is listening to the dog's heart sounds and breathing.

It is time for the dog to go to the **veterinarian** again. The vet makes sure that she is healthy.

Newborn

6 weeks

2 months

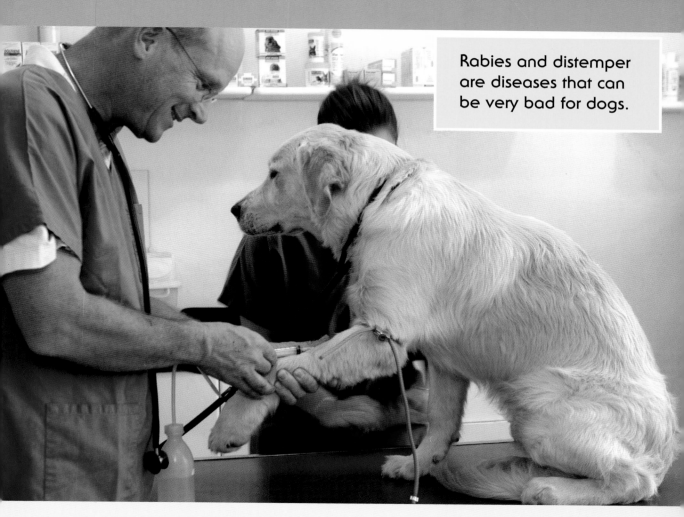

Rabies and distemper are diseases that can be very bad for dogs.

A vet will give the dog a **booster shot** to make sure she does not get sick. The vet will also clip the dog's nails so they do not get too long.

1 year

3 years

8 years

3 Years

Male and female golden retrievers look very similar. Males are usually a bit bigger.

The dog's owner wants her to have puppies of her own. She is taken to meet a **male** dog and they **mate**.

Newborn

6 weeks

2 months

Puppies are ready to be born about 63 days after mating.

Now several new puppies are growing inside her. Look how big her stomach is! She is almost ready to give birth.

1 year

3 years

8 years

9 Weeks After Mating

Puppies in the same litter are called littermates.

The dog gives birth to her **litter** of puppies one by one. The puppies are very small. They feed on her milk and grow quickly.

Newborn

6 weeks

2 months

The coats on golden retriever puppies get longer as they get older.

By the time they are three weeks old the puppies can bark and wag their tails. At three months old the puppies are ready to go to new owners.

1 year

3 years

8 years

5 Years

Golden retrievers may go white around the face as they get older.

The dog misses her puppies for a few days, but then she forgets about them. She goes back to her old life with her owners.

Newborn

6 weeks

2 months

Golden retrievers like to swim and play in water.

The dog's owners take her for long walks. When they throw a stick she runs after it. She may swim through water to fetch the stick.

1 year

3 years

8 years

It's a Dog's Life

An older dog may need special food to keep it from gaining weight.

The dog is eight years old now. She still needs exercise every day, but she walks more slowly now and does not run around like before.

Newborn

6 weeks

2 months

Most dogs live until they are ten to fifteen years old. Small dogs often live longer than bigger dogs.

A dog can be your friend for a long time.

1 year

3 years

8 years

Life Cycle

Newborn

6 weeks

2 months

1 year

3 years

8 years

Fact File

- Dogs are **popular** pets. There are around 75 million pet dogs in the United States.

- Retrievers have a waterproof undercoat. They like being in water.

- A dog has such a good sense of smell, it can smell and track people from the footprints left by their shoes.

- Retrievers can have several **litters**. In each litter they usually have seven to nine puppies.

Glossary

booster second shot to make the first shot work better

energy ability to run around and do things

female girl

guide dog dog that is trained to help people with sight problems find their way around

litter several baby animals born together

male boy

mate when a male and a female come together to produce babies

popular liked by many people

shot special liquid that is injected into the body to help prevent an illness

teat part of a female animal's body that puppies suck milk through

trained taught

veterinarian animal doctor

More Books to Read

Ganeri, Anita. *A Pet's Life: Dog.* Chicago: Heinemann Library, 2009.

Whitehouse, Patricia. *Pets in My House: Dog.* Chicago: Heinemann Library, 2004.

Index